# BORN TO OVERCOME

WILEY JACKSON, JR.

# BORN TO OVERCOME

## WILEY JACKSON, JR.

Tulsa, Oklahoma

BORN TO OVERCOME

*Born to Overcome* by Wiley Jackson, Jr.
Published by Insight Publishing Group
8801 S. Yale, Suite 410
Tulsa, OK 74137
918-493-1718

This book or parts thereof may not be reproduced in any form, stored in a retrieval system, or transmitted in any form by any means—electronic, mechanical, photocopy, recording, or otherwise—without prior written permission of the publisher, except as provided by United States copyright law.

Unless otherwise noted, all Scripture quotations are from the New King James Version of the Bible. Copyright © 1979, 1980, 1982 by Thomas Nelson, Inc., publishers. Scripture quotations marked NIV are from the New International Version of the Bible. Copyright © 1973, 1978, 1984 by International Bible Society. Used by permission of Zondervan Publishing House.

Copyright © 2003 by Wiley Jackson, Jr.
All rights reserved.

ISBN 1-930027-76-1
Library of Congress catalog card number:2002114021

Printed in the United States of America

# Dedication

I dedicate this book to my wife, Mary, my sons, Wiley III and Paul Emerson and all the people who have sown into my life and have believed in me over the last twenty years. Without the constant drive from those of you who draw strength from my anointing, loyalty, and integrity in God, I would have given up a long time ago. So, I never cease to make mention of you in my prayers.

Thank you for your continuous support. May God's blessings be upon you as we carry out His will and journey into another frontier.

# Contents

Dedication

Foreword

Introduction

Chapter One: Overcomers                    29

Chapter Two: Born to Overcome              35

Chapter Three: Calling Individuals         43

Chapter Four: Climbing the Mountain        47

Chapter Five: Foundation Check             51

Conclusion

# Foreword

When God birthed this book in my spirit, I couldn't help but think back on the things my mother had told me about my childhood. She told how she had to trust God when her first-born's life seemed to be slipping away. This became a personal look at my belief that we were *Born to Overcome*.

It all began when I was about eighteen-months-old. According to my mother, I had always been a happy baby—eager to get up in the morning and playful all day long. But one morning, something was different. She called for me to get up out of bed with her daily chant, "Come to mommy, come to mommy now," and I just stared. So, she thought she'd do a second round of the chant. Again, I just stared.

After a few days of declining energy, my mother decided to take me to the doctor. At that time we couldn't just jump in the car and head to the doctor's office. We had no car; so we had to ride the bus. Once we arrived and the doctor looked me over, he told my mother that he needed to run some tests. So he sent us back home and mentioned that my mother should bring my father back with her. My mother phoned my father, who came home early from work, and they both anxiously waited on "the" call. When "the" call finally came in, the nurse instructed my mother to bring me back into the office and to bring along my father. What nervousness this must have caused a young 20-year-old mother who also had a 3-month-old and was pregnant with a third child.

She and my father took me back into the doctor's office, and it was there that doctors explained that I had all of the symptoms of Leukemia but they needed to admit me into the hospital for more observations. My parents had never heard of Leukemia; and my mother surely had no intentions of going back home without me. But she had no choice.

However, she did have one choice—whether or not to learn more about this Leukemia thing. And she chose to go to the library, where she gathered enough information to send her into a depression. The books implied that there was no cure and that I would probably not live. But my mother continued to visit me in the hospital with hopes that the books had no merit.

One day, while in the waiting room, my mother met an old woman who asked her why she was there. My mother began telling the woman about her woes. And though my mother didn't know this woman—and still doesn't know her name or why she was there—she took this stranger's advice. The woman told my mother to pray daily, "Lord, let your will be done, and I'll be satisfied." My mother prayed that prayer everyday, but she would add, "Lord, if you let my baby live, I promise I'll give him back to you."

After four months in two different hospitals, along with numerous tests and experimental medications, I began showing signs of that happy baby again. And during that time, my mother saw that old woman again who asked how I was doing. My mother told her that I was getting much better. In fact, the doctors had changed their diagnosis from Leukemia to "Pernicious Anemia" (whatever that is). I was released from the hospital; and as a true sign that I was back on track, I ate a whole box of Ritz Crackers on the way home!

But before I left the hospital the old woman said to my mother, "I knew he would get better; and someday he will do great things and will travel all over the world."

Well, I've certainly done some great things in God and have traveled to more places than I had ever imagined. I now know that I was truly *Born to Overcome*.

So as you read this book, know that you too were *Born to Overcome*. Your life is not your own . . .

# Introduction

My career as a pastor started with a lot of enthusiasm, but I had the wrong vision. In late 1982, I was sitting on my bed at home and watching a famous evangelist on television. At the time, I was a frustrated church member. As I watched, I said, "I can do better than that on my off days."

Just then God spoke to me. "You have one problem, Wiley. He's preaching and you're sitting here on the bed."

Those words stirred me into action. The next week I started looking until I found a storefront. I rented it even though I didn't have a single member or know anyone who would come to the church. But I felt I had to do it because I had a strong desire in my spirit to build a church for God.

A lot of people asked me, "Did God tell you to go to that particular store front?"

"No. I rented it," I answered them, "because it was the cheapest place I could find." It was located at the Parkview Plaza Shopping Center in Southeast Atlanta and cost me $250 a month. For $300, I could pay the rent as well as the light bill and the gas. I worked for Frito Lay, so I knew I could swing that much money. On top of the monthly payments, I borrowed $1,500 so I could put in seats and a small pulpit.

I began to preach at what I then called the Gospel Tabernacle Deliverance Center and trusted God that the people would come in. And they did – one by one.

When I began it was frightening. I had no one by my side. I had a lot of friends who thought they helped by telling me what they believed was best for me. "It's not the will of God," was the advice most often.

More than one looked at me and said, "You've got to be crazy."

Starting a church was a big undertaking. Finally, I said, "Well, Lord, if it doesn't work, I can always continue with my job."

From the first day it was exciting. I loved to preach about Jesus Christ, even if nobody came to listen. What a joy it was when people did listen. By the end of the first year I had twelve members. Twelve whole members. Five of them were from my family, but they were members. I hadn't become a big-time pastor, but I was doing God's will, and it was exciting.

I did just about everything in those days. For instance, sometimes the whole church went on trips to sing and preach. We could put all our members into one van, and I'd drive. Once we got to our destination, I'd check all the equipment, set it up, and then run into a back room, change clothes, and preach the sermon. After the sermon was over I'd change clothes again, take down the equipment, put it into the van, and drive the people back home. A lot of work, but I loved it.

I didn't complain because I was too thrilled about what God was doing. It may not sound like much to some people, but with those twelve members, I felt I had become a success in the ministry. I also knew it was just the beginning. By the end of the second year, we had twenty-four members.

Now I was finally a big-time pastor. We needed two vans to carry all the church members. We were growing, and I had visions of fifty, a hundred, even two hundred people worshipping together.

It didn't work that way. I can think of two major reasons I didn't progress after that. First, I still had a lot of doubts about God calling me to be a pastor. Maybe it was because I wanted to preach so badly and didn't have the needed confidence. But I struggled with that question for a long time.

My second problem was that I didn't know how to exercise leadership. Rather than taking responsibility and asserting myself, I often put off making a decision or let someone else do it. One time I said to the members, "I believe God is telling us to buy another van." But I didn't know how to proceed, so I asked, "What do you have to say?"

"We don't need another van," somebody complained.

"You're probably right," I said. "It's not time to buy a van." I knew in my spirit that God was telling me to do it. But I gave in to the negative voices and failed to exercise leadership.

Near the end of the second year, we had a church split. I lost twelve of the members—twelve of the good-paying members—and it cut our membership in half. I felt like David in the days when he ran from King Saul, left with only those who were in debt, distressed, or discontented.

After the twelve members left, I went home totally depressed. I wasn't married at that time, so I really was alone. I had failed God, the people, and myself. I cried out, "God, I didn't ask for this in the first place. I've still got a good job. I'll just go to work and forget this church idea."

I told myself I'd never go back to the Gospel Tabernacle. I'd never be a preacher again. It had been stupid to think I could lead a growing church. Yet even as I told God those things, I knew I wanted to preach more than anything else.

The next day, my father who wasn't saved at that time, came to me. "I heard what happened to you."

"I don't want to talk about it. You don't understand church business."

"I may not understand church business, Son, but I know one thing, and you need to know it too. You are the pastor. No matter what goes on in that church, you are responsible."

"I don't want to hear that. I'm not responsible. They did me wrong. They lied and betrayed me. They let me down. I didn't ask for this."

Yeah, I know," he said, "but you're still responsible. If you work at it, you can continue, Son."

He talked some more, even though I didn't like what he said. After he left, I kept thinking about his words. No matter how I tried, I couldn't get away from what he had said. Then I realized something I'd never forget: the people who left weren't to blame. My father was right; I had denied my responsibility. I hadn't led them, so one of the deacons had done what I wouldn't do. He took the leadership role on just about everything. When he left, they followed their leader.

It took a while, but God used those words from my dad to turn me around. If I didn't lead, someone else would. I decided I had to go back to the storefront church and take responsibility for the ministry God had called me to.

"I can do it," I said, with a confidence I had never felt before.

From that bad experience I learned that it's important for a pastor or anybody thinking about going into ministry to be assured of the call. When they're assured of the call, they can assume leadership, and they can trust God. During those first two years, I hadn't had the assurance I needed. I got it only after losing those twelve members.

Before the church split, my young brother, Rodney, had come into the church. Even though he was capable, I didn't want him as the assistant pastor because he was my brother. I didn't want people to say, "The only reason Rodney is the assistant pastor is because he's Wiley's brother." To avoid that, I tried other men, but they never worked out. When I started over, I decided that as soon as I needed an assistant, Rodney would be the one.

God told me to go back to the church and have a Praise-a-thon, and I said, "Yes, Lord." This time I didn't ask anyone's opinion; this time I told them what God had told me.

"This is what we're going to do. For the next thirty days, I'm going to minister on only one thing; praising the Lord," I said as I looked right at them. "I'm not going to talk about the people who left. I'm not going to talk about how bad they were. I'm only going to talk about Jesus and how good he is!"

"Praise the Lord," was the first comment I heard.

I began to lead the people; we praised the Lord every day and in everything. Even with all the praising, things didn't miraculously turn around. In fact, we faced terrible problems. The church roof began to leak. We praised the Lord for giving us a building while we worked hard to raise the money to repair it. The van broke down, and for a long time we didn't have the money to have it fixed. We praised the Lord that we had a van at all and praised him for the next one we were going to buy.

By the end of those thirty days, we had started the church's third year. I had exercised my leadership, I had done what God had told me to do, and God honored my obedience. I couldn't believe how quickly the situation turned around. God started sending new people to the church.

"How did you hear about the church?" we asked the new people.

"I really don't know," was the way the answer usually started. One woman said, "I just got off the bus out on Memorial Drive and saw there was a church here in the shopping center."

"Somebody told me about this church," one man said. "I didn't know who the guy was. He said he didn't go to your church, but it was a good one, and he thought I'd like it here."

Our church was located in the middle of a shopping center on a busy Atlanta street. On one side of us was a bingo parlor and on the other was the Mellow Fellow Nightclub. Sometimes I'd be preaching and I'd hear, "B-5," followed by a loud yell, "Bingo!" in the middle of my message.

On the other side of our church was the nightclub. They would start playing rhythm and blues music. Many of us had come out of that lifestyle, but we still remembered the music. It was hard for me to stand in my pulpit and try to preach when I'd hear one of my favorite R&B songs through the walls.

The members would try to listen to me, but all the time, they were patting their feet in time to the music. "Praise the Lord," I'd cry out and hope God would distract them from the music.

Despite things like that, God continued to bring in new people. So many came I needed an assistant, and I knew God wanted Rodney. (After Rodney became the assistant pastor, he went to Beulah Heights Bible College, graduated, and went on to the Interdenominational Theological Center for his master's degree in theology. He also taught at Beulah Heights. In 1997, the students and faculty voted him Teacher of the Year.)

The more I exercised leadership, the more the ministry grew. One day in 1985, I had a vision. I saw a church building. It just floated down out of the sky. It was a real vision, not just a thought. The doors opened, and it was as if a camera panned the sanctuary while it went through the doors. I could see everything that was happening. I saw myself preaching in the pulpit, and the place was full of people listening and praising God.

"Oh, Lord, that can't be me." I think I was too overwhelmed at first to believe that could be me with that kind of church.

Yet I knew it was God. In fact, I was so sure, I talked to an architect that same week and told him what I had seen. He worked with me and drew up plans to build the kind of church building I had seen in the vision.

I went back and told our members, "We're going to build a new church." At that time we had only seventy-five members, but I felt like a full-blown, national pastor and big-time evangelist. My dreams were large, and they were all going to happen right away.

I had received a vision and just rushed right into it, but I didn't do any research on the building costs. "We're going to build this huge church," I told the member, "and I believe it will cost us two hundred thousand dollars. God said we could raise two hundred thousand to build it."

By now they were used to me exercising leadership, and no one argued.

A few weeks later, I brought in a bonding company to handle the financing of the church. We would have to raise the money by selling bonds for them to loan us the money to pay for the construction. The bonding company and the lenders earned interest, so it was like working with a bank, except that we had to sell the bonds ourselves.

From then on, at every service I said, "God says as soon as we get two hundred thousand dollars, we can build." I didn't even have the final plans; I just had a picture in my mind. I figured that the money we raised would get a building up. After we got inside to worship, we could finish the rest of it ourselves.

We continued to pray and raise the money. No matter how hard we worked, it seemed as if we could never raise two hundred thousand dollars. Something always happened. Once, the roof started to leak, and we couldn't sit there with water dripping in. We had to fix the hole in the roof.

Despite all the setbacks, I didn't get discouraged. "These walls must fall," I'd say. "We're going to conquer the devil! This is the will of God, and we're going to make it happen!"

We didn't make it happen. Time ran out for us to raise the money for the bond program. We had the land in our name – even though it wasn't paid for – but that's about all we had.

I had failed again. Depression and self-pity hit me. "What's wrong with me?" I asked God. "I tried to lead, and I led to failure." I knew I had to get up in front of those people and say, "I missed God this time."

It was difficult, but I did it. I had to. "This just isn't the Lord's will." I said. "I believe it is God's will for us to build, but I didn't have the timing right. I got off on the wrong vision about building the church. You know, a lot of times God is talking to you and lot of other voices are talking to you. The devil talks to you. And God is talking too."

"How do we know when it's God's voice?" one of the members asked.

"It's like choosing doors. You open door number one, and it's not right. So you close it and put an X on it, and you know not to go back to door number one anymore." I paused and knew I had to tell them I had failed.

"Through the process of elimination is how we know what's right. I've been checking those doors, and I found the two-hundred-thousand-dollar door and opened it, but it wasn't the right one." Again I paused and looked at them before I added, "I'll never listen to that voice again. I put an X on that door. But there is a right door in God. And when we open it, everything will go just like God said."

As I continued to preach that morning, I told them they needed to understand that I was only a human being, a man God uses. "However, I am also a man that misses God on various issues." Then I told them plainly that I had missed God.

"Whew, Pastor, I'm glad you said that," said one of the men. "For a while we were thinking you weren't like us.

They understood. They forgave me, and I felt their love. My failing at choosing that bond program helped me to realize that I'm not God. I often tell my people that when we start acting like God, we take on Godlike problems. Nobody can handle Godlike problems but God himself. When we are under God, then it's up to him to handle the Godlike problems.

That experience of failure changed my ministry. Since then, one policy I have put in place at Gospel Tabernacle is that whenever something happens right or wrong, the pastor will get up and address it. I will tell them what I did, and what happened, and what we're going to do about it.

To my amazement, when the people accepted that I had failed, it didn't affect my leadership. I told them I still believed it was God's will for us to build, but it would happen in God's way and with God's timing.

Then I backtracked to do things right. First, I had plans drawn up for the church. We raised twenty-four thousand to pay the architect for them. We didn't have money to build, but we made ourselves ready for God's timing. We talked to different companies about constructing a building, even though we still didn't have money.

I went to every bank in Atlanta and asked for a loan for one million dollars – the true cost to build what I had seen in my vision. Without exception, they turned me down.

At the last bank I sat down to talk to the loan officer. He wasn't very friendly to begin with. Then when I showed him our financial records, he shook his head. "Do you mean to tell me you think you can borrow this much money to build a church with these finances?"

He could have turned us down nicely the way others had, but he was just plain mean. I left with my feelings hurt.

"They've all turned us down," I said to Rodney with tears in my eyes, "but I believe someone in the United States of America is going to lend us the money to build a church."

Both of us knew it wouldn't be a bank in Atlanta.

A construction firm in Greenville, South Carolina advertised in *Pulpit Helps* magazine. "We build churches," the ad read. At that time, Rodney worked for Eastern Airlines and had a family pass, so we could fly free. Rodney and I flew up to see them.

In the middle of showing our plans, the headman said, "There's a company in Alabama that provides money for congregations to build churches. We usually charge twenty thousand dollars for this information but there's something about you guys I like, so I'm telling it to you free."

We had just met him, and we believed it was God that made him come forth with that information. He explained that the company helped churches through the bond issue, but this one was different. The company itself sold all the bonds.

Rodney and I flew straight from Greenville to Alabama. When we got there the man was too busy to talk to us, but he did say we could see him in Atlanta the following week. His company had a representative in Atlanta that he was going to meet with. As it turned out, an emergency came up so that I couldn't meet with him and neither could Rodney. Our church's administrator, Melvin Drake, went to meet him.

We didn't know it then, but the Atlanta representative had once worked for Melvin and liked him. That man set up a meeting with one of the vice presidents of the company. We took our financial information to him and said, " We want to borrow a million dollars for the church."

We knew our financial statement didn't stand up to our paying back a million dollars. He looked it over. Then he said, "Yes, Pastor Jackson, you can do it. We can get you the money, and you can build the church. Will sixty days be okay?"

"Sixty days would be fine," I said, so overwhelmed I could hardly get the words out. "That's just right on schedule."

Rodney and I have often said that for those sixty days, that man and his family were safe as they'd ever be in their lives because we prayed for them fervently every day and fasted regularly. "Lord, don't let him have an accident," we prayed. "Don't let him even get sick. Don't let anything bad happen to him before we get our money."

As excited as I was, I kept thinking, it can't be this easy. Something will happen to make it fail.

The company sent the money.

Rodney and I went to the very bank where the man had hurt my feelings. "I hope you remember me," I said. "You turned us down when we wanted to borrow money. Today I'm here because we want to open a checking account."

"Oh, yes, yes, I do remember you." He looked at me in a sarcastic way, and I knew he was thinking, *Oh, you're back again.* "How much do you want to deposit to open the account?"

"One million dollars."

He stared at me and then at the check I held in my hand. "Oh, yes, Reverend Jackson, we can help you!" He gave me the biggest smile he was capable of. "Just sit right down here." He pointed to chairs for us to sit in. "Yes, just sit down, and we'll fill out the papers."

He opened the account and gave me a temporary checkbook. When I got up, he extended his hand. "So good to do business with you, Reverend Jackson."

I took his hand, shook it, and said, "Sir, never mess with a child of God."

He smiled sheepishly, and I knew I had made my point. Since then, whenever I see him, I go out of my way to talk to him. He'll always respond, "Reverend, whatever you say is all right."

It took us a full year, but we built Gospel Tabernacle, and as we like to say, "The rest is his story."

When we started to build, we still had seventy-five members and met for another year in that tiny building. We experienced no growth during that time. Doubts would start to come, but I'd remind myself that God had provided the money, and God would do whatever it took to fill up the new building.

We moved into the church in 1987. Immediately the growth began. Now, we hold two services and see fifteen hundred members every Sunday.

It took nearly seven years to pay off the million dollars. Since that time we've enlarged and redone some things, and we've added another two-million-dollar addition to the church.

Despite my failures, God had given me a vision, and God fulfilled the vision.

*Born to Overcome* is Pastor Jackson's first book, and it helps celebrate his twentieth year in the ministry. It is his prayer that this book reaches the world and helps transform lives and change destinies.

*Born to Overcome* strives to help believers practically apply the Word of God to their every- day living and to reinforce Pastor Jackson's belief that we all are born to overcome. Pastor Jackson uses a simple approach to awaken the Spirit and to touch both the young and old, transcending all ethnic origins.

## Chapter One

# Overcomers

It is an immutable fact that we will face many obstacles throughout our lifetimes, and these obstacles will either keep us from growing or make us press forward; we give up, or we get going. I believe that God desires that we overcome our obstacles and launch out with our dreams. 1 John 5:4 gives us a promise: "For everyone born of God overcomes the world. This is the victory that has overcome the world, even our faith."

Let's look at the word *overcome*. Webster's definition of *overcome* is "to conquer, to master, to prevail over, to surmount, or to overpower." As I looked more at the meaning of the word, I thought about some of my favorite role models—past and present—who overcame obstacles that threatened their very lives. I want you to take a moment to share some of my favorite examples of people that overcame significant odds and disadvantages and succeeded despite their difficulties.

> I believe that God desires that we overcome our obstacles and launch out with our dreams.

Wilma Rudolph was born two months prematurely, weighing only four and a half pounds. The twentieth of twenty-two children, she battled measles, mumps, and chicken pox all before age four. At age four, she nearly died fighting pneumonia and scarlet fever. Her mother noticed a problem with her left leg after she had recovered from that trial. Doctors later diagnosed it as polio and said her chances for recovering the full use of her leg were slim. Rudolph wore a leg brace and traveled with her mother fifty miles each way by bus twice a week to the Meharry Medical College in Nashville, Tennessee, for treatment. By age twelve, she had begun walking without the brace. Despite all of these obstacles, Wilma Rudolph never gave up. Later, she won several gold medals in track and field at the Olympics, gaining the title "Fastest Woman in the World." Jesse Owens, another track star, also struggled with physical ailments in his younger years. Already thin and frail, he nearly lost his life while suffering four consecutive bouts of pneumonia. Owens' high school coach encouraged him to run to strengthen his lungs for the northern winters in Cleveland, Ohio. That same strength pushed him beyond his obstacles to break ten Olympic track records and tie two other records in the 1936 Olympics in Berlin.

Stevie Wonder was born blind. His mother raised him and his five siblings after separating from his father. She took Stevie to several doctors, hoping he would someday see, only to be disappointed. His musical talent, however, began to gain prominence. He received his first harmonica at age five and a drum at age nine. By the time he was twelve, he had written and recorded a song that

> By the time Stevie Wonder was twelve, he had written and recorded a song that resulted in the sale of over one and a half million records.

resulted in the sale of over one and a half million records. Stevie Wonder is still one of the most respected composers and musicians in the world.

Les Brown's life was very interesting to me. He was born into poverty, adopted, and was raised by a single mother and labeled "educable but mentally retarded." Brown also suffered diphtheria at a young age. And although the infectious disease claimed the lives of several of his neighborhood friends, Brown survived with the aid of medicine and his Mamma's prayers. He didn't let the label and illness overcome him. In fact, he used them as motivation. Les started out as a disc jockey, then a community activist, and then rose to serve three terms in the Ohio State Legislature. Today, he is a renowned motivational speaker and author.

Maya Angelou, a great poet and public speaker, was raped by her mother's boyfriend when she was eight. She had a child when she was sixteen. Angelou has overcome her unfavorable childhood and is now a best-selling author. Her poetic address at the 1993 inauguration ceremony for President Bill Clinton touched the lives of millions.

Of course, there are many others who turned trials into opportunities. Some rose to higher heights simply because someone said they wouldn't make it. Others used their stumbling blocks to build great monuments, and some planted only one tree but produced a mighty forest.

Having heard of these success stories, let me ask, are we born to overcome or to fail? Are we people that are destined to succeed or concede? As you read, keep these questions in mind.

I want you to take a moment to stop and think. I want you to remember a time when you were so consumed by a trial, a difficulty, or a dilemma that you could not see beyond it—where it dominated your vision. Maybe you almost gave up on life, but if you're reading this, you didn't. Thank God! I'd say, then, that if you're reading this, you were born to overcome.

> Are we born to overcome or to fail? Are we people that are destined to succeed or concede?

## Chapter Two

# Born to Overcome

Gregor Yohann Mendel, the father of modern genetics, discovered that each individual is the sum total of his parents. This means that you possess all of your mother and father's genetic potential. Whether the genes are dominant or recessive, all of them—from both parents—were passed on to you. You may act more like your father but possess your mother's physical traits, or you may look more like your mother but have the same type of hair or eye color as your father. However they have emerged, you have the genes they both passed on to you—your genetic inheritance.

Now, just as you inherit traits from your parents, you inherit traits from your Father God when you are born again. However, from Him you inherit *invincible* genes! When you get God's invincible seed, it means you become incapable of being conquered, overcome, or subdued. You receive an overcoming heritage when you enter into God's family by turning your life over to Him, believing in your heart, and confessing with your mouth that Jesus Christ is Lord!

The Bible has a lot to say about our opportunities to overcome when we become born again. 1 John 5:4-5 says, "For everyone born of God overcomes the world. This is the victory that has overcome the world, even our faith. Who is it that overcomes the world? Only he who believes that Jesus is the Son of God."

> When you get God's invincible seed, it means you become incapable of being conquered, overcome, or subdued.

I still vividly remember the joy I felt when I gave my life to Jesus Christ. I was very nervous when I jumped out of my seat, ran to the altar, and said the words, "I believe that Jesus Christ is the Son of God, and I accept him as Lord and Savior over my life." Those words represented a commitment I made, an understanding that I needed Jesus in my life and that I wanted to do whatever it took to have a personal relationship with Him. In that moment, I inherited invincible seed—God genes.

You see, the Church is a type of mother, and believers are the egg! Then one day, the Father's seed enters the Church, where it finds you open and waiting. When the Father deposits that seed—when you are born again—He imparts to you all of His genes. You become a new creation that possesses all of God's traits and has incredible Godly potential—and that's powerful potential!

You have a choice in determining which traits are dominant and which are recessive. You walked into church with a genetic aptitude for sin the day you were saved, and its lineage is still within you, but within you now also exists the invincible seed that you received from God. You have your choice: the traits with which you were born or the traits with which you were born again.

*You, dear children, are from God
and have overcome them,
because the one who is in you is greater
than the one who is in the world.*
I John 4:4

First John 4:4 reminds us that we have the power within us to overcome. By understanding that you have new genes, you also can know and understand who you are. You don't have to stumble and fall on your way up the mountain as you used to; it's now in your genetic makeup to be predisposed to making it all the way to the top! It's in your genes to resist the devil, to get up, and to stay up. It will now be easier for you to grab on to faith, because faith is now within you, flowing through your veins.

Praise is also within you! You have a Godly ability to worship and commune with Him, and it isn't learned behavior; it's within you, part of you, because it's now part of your makeup as a new creature in Christ. It's in you, and you will—must!—give God the glory!

All you must do to experience these and innumerable other traits is to activate them and make them dominant. They're in you.

Now that you've been introduced to your Godly, indomitable genes, you must also understand that we're in a constant struggle with the devil. And one reason we still wrestle—and at times feel defeated by the devil—is that we're not equipped to handle defeat.

Let me explain: God never knew defeat. *Never*. And since we now have His genes, we can't handle defeat. Our spirit says we're not supposed to experience defeat, because God has given us the power to overcome.

The devil is the father of lies, a perpetrator of false truth: he might tell you that you'll never reach a particular goal, and a part of you might reason that it's true; it seems unlikely you will reach that goal. However, instead of listening to that interpretation of things, shake your finger at him and say, "Yes I can! It's in me! I can do all things through Christ who strengthens me!" He might tell you that you can't make it; you tell him, "Yes I can! It's in me!" He'll often try to make you think you can't possibly overcome the situation you're in, but again he's wrong. You *can*. God has given you the power—it is now part of who you are!

Satan is the accuser of the brethren; he brings charges against us before God and makes sure there are plenty of charges to be made. Revelation 12:10 says the devil is going to be cast down and that he's been accusing us before God day and night. It tells us what's going to happen, so when he tells you that you're not going to overcome, tell him he has it the wrong way around—he's the one that won't overcome *you*!

> When *your* back is against the wall, remember: you have His overcoming genes in you!

As have so many others, I have experienced many tough trials in my life, but in the midst of it all, God spoke to me and said, "Wiley, it's *in* you!"

When *your* back is against the wall, remember: you have His overcoming genes in you! You have power within you that won't let you quit, power that won't let you take adversity lying down.

The invincible seed within you will cause you to rise in the midst of difficult circumstances and say, "I was *born* to overcome!"

## CHAPTER THREE

# CALLING INDIVIDUALS

I believe that everyone is born to fulfill a divine calling. Even before you were born, God had a plan for your life. It is important that you get to know what God's vision—His plan, His divine calling—is for your life.

I remember when I first realized that God's vision for me was to be a preacher. My reaction then was, "Oh no, Lord, not me! No way!" It took some time before I actively pursued His vision for me, but now that I have been for years, I can't see my life having taken any other turn and still being as perfectly suited to me.

In our pursuit for His vision, we must be careful that we not try to clone the purpose He has given to the people around us. People often want to be like someone else, someone they admire. Popular actors often act like someone they admire, singers try to imitate other singers, and some preachers are trying to be the same as other preachers! I've heard sermons preached by two different people on the exact same thing exactly the same way. That's attempting to clone another individual!

But God is not calling for clones. He is calling for individuals. God calls us to do something special, and He's calling for you to be somebody for Him. Find out His will for your life and live up to the call!

> God is not calling for clones. He is calling for individuals. God calls us to do something special, and He's calling for you to be somebody for Him. Find out His will for your life and live up to the call!

Acting is a natural part of being human—we do it before we're saved, and some people do it after. If you're not careful, you can bring that same spirit into the Church with you. Every one of us has at one time or another acted in a certain way to get someone to like us or to get something we wanted. We've performed to belong; we've done things a certain way to keep the pressure off or put it on someone else.

However, instead of behaving the same way someone else does, try sitting still. God will let you know His divine calling for you—the real you, not the actor in you. God is not calling for actors, He's calling for individuals! Be yourself; God called you, and He's created you anew in His image now that you're born again. If you listen, He will tell you the truth—the truth about who you are in Him.

*Jesus said, "If you hold to my teaching,*
*you are really my disciples. Then you will know*
*the truth and the truth will set you free."*
John 8:31-32

## CHAPTER FOUR

# CLIMBING THE MOUNTAIN

*Let your eyes look straight ahead, fix your gaze directly before you. Make level paths for your feet and take only ways that are firm.*
Proverbs 4:25-26

    The Bible tells us that the Lord orders the steps of a good man. God knows the path we are going to take before we do. He guides our steps!

    Throughout the Bible, from the very first pages of Genesis to the last pages of Revelation, God gives His people the same loving, timeless message: "Don't give up! Keep trusting Me! I will bring you through any difficulty. I will make you victorious in life!"

Throughout the Word, He encourages and inspires humanity, knowing that His creation will face challenging obstacles in life from time to time. And because of the challenges and opposition we face, there's probably not one person who hasn't at one time or another thought, "What's the use? I might as well give up!"

Look into the Bible; you will see examples of people who faced opportunities to quit at times when everything appeared to be against them. It's encouraging to our faith to look at them and see how their faith in God brought them out.

> Don't allow your circumstances to daunt your faith. When confronted with impossibilities, don't give up!

They were ordinary people who didn't allow circumstances to daunt their faith. They were not necessarily great men and women, but they were men and women who had great faith in a great God. When they were confronted with impossibilities, they didn't just give up. They held on to their faith in God.

I like to compare walking with the Lord to climbing a large mountain. When we are born again, we are at the base of the mountain. The area is flat and safe for a newborn to explore. As we grow in the Lord, we climb into the foothills. The foothills are a little taller, a little steeper, but still relatively easy to climb. When we get careless—as most do—we might lose our balance or footing and slide back down the mountain.

Some people shake it off and immediately start to climb back up. They may take the same path they took the last time, remember the slippery area, sidestep around it, and keep on going. Others will take an entirely different path back up that mountain to bypass the dangerous area altogether.

But then there are those of us who trudge right back up the same path, hit the same area, and fall back down again. It might not be as far this time, though some fall back even farther. Some people fall and give up; they sit still and never try to climb again.

As we continue to grow, we still climb the mountain. It has more peaks and valleys and more sharp edges and trials to encounter. And it doesn't matter who you are, everyone encounters slippery spots and rough edges. How you handle them is what's important.

Along the way, God provides resting areas—plateaus—for us. We can rest there and plan the next stretch of our journey. We can look back down the mountain into our past—not to judge or get angry—but to rejoice in the progress we've made.

Always remember that when you're in a tight spot or when you encounter a slippery area, God will elevate you from where you are in your climb to where you *should* be.

Keep climbing the mountain! You are destined to overcome!

> Always remember that when you're in a tight spot or when you encounter a slippery area, God will elevate you from where you are in your climb to where you *should* be.

## CHAPTER FIVE

# FOUNDATION CHECK

Now that you know you were born to overcome, that you have invincible seed and a divine calling and that you're equipped to climb life's mountains, it's time to evaluate the foundation of your Christian life. It's time to make sure you've taken the necessary steps to be saved.

Many times people don't survive trials because they didn't follow the right steps. But if you keep following the steps that are ordered by the Lord, regardless of how dark or difficult it is, He will meet you at the top. Steps take you higher, and God can elevate you from where you are to where you should be.

The Bible tells us, "For it is with your heart that you believe and are justified, and it is with

> Many times people don't survive trials because they didn't follow the right steps. But if you keep following the steps that are ordered by the Lord, regardless of how dark or difficult it is, He will meet you at the top.

your mouth that you confess and are saved," in Romans 10:10.

If you haven't gone through the following process in your life, get started today. You will never be the same.

Here are some steps and some specific points that you might find useful!

## Step One: Turn Your Life Over to Christ

Turning your life over to Christ involves a few main points, which are the basics of salvation.

You must *admit* that you are a sinner. Sin is always an offense toward God. Whether you sin against yourself or against someone else, it offends God. Romans 3:23 reminds us "all have sinned and fall short of the glory of God."

*Repent* of your sins. This means more than just feeling sorry that you did something wrong.

The word *repent* means "to turn around completely." Quit blaming everyone else for your sin! Take responsibility for your own actions and attitudes, and make up your mind to turn away from sin. Then *do it*! The Holy Spirit will help you.

You must *believe* that Jesus died on the cross for you and that He arose from the dead. Through this, He bore all of our sins. We should've died for our sins, but God loves us so much that He sent His Son to become a sacrifice for us! Hebrews 12:2 says, "Let us fix our eyes on Jesus, the author and perfecter of our faith, who for the joy set before him endured the cross, scorning its shame, and sat down at the right hand of the throne of God."

However, all of these choices mean nothing if you don't *receive* Jesus into your life. Just ask Him to come in and live in your heart. Tell Jesus you want to give Him full control of your life. He will then become your Savior and the Lord of your life.

**Step Two: Practice! Practice! Practice!**

*Testify*. Tell someone who knows you very well that you have made a commitment to Jesus Christ. Private promises are too easy to break! By telling your family that you are born again, you put your vow on record. From then on, they will be watching you to see if your confession and commitment are real.

*Read the Word.* Your Bible will become your closest friend. This is your love letter from God. Keep your Bible with you at all times, and take time to read it every day. Before you open it, ask the Lord to make it clear to you and make it alive that day. He will! Start with five minutes and increase gradually. Write in it, and underline what stands out to you.

*Prayer* is your private conversation with God. Spend time just talking to Him as you would talk to a friend. If you're angry, or if you hate someone or something, tell Him. Be yourself. Be honest. God loves you just the way you are; He'll get you where you need to be in due time.

*Praise* the Lord all day long. Make Him your focal point throughout the day. Thank Him for His goodness! Sing songs to Him! Love Him! Adore Him! Thank Him and praise Him from in the morning when you first wake until before you go to bed. Psalms 113:3 says, "From the rising of the sun to the place where it sets, the name of the Lord is to be praised."

## Step Three: Join with Other Believers

*Find a church*—find one that's right for you. God has already prepared a place and purpose for you in the Body of Christ. Ask Him now to guide you to your church home. Your church should be a place where the Bible is taught and preached. It will be a big part of your new lifestyle. God has chosen for you new brothers and sisters to surround you, to support you, and to show you how to love. Also, if you are to walk successfully in your new Christian life, you must listen to, learn from, and obey your pastor. He is the watchman over your soul.

I believe that you should *pray to be filled with the Holy Spirit*. Make sure that your church believes in being filled with the Holy Spirit with the evidence of speaking in tongues, which is God's promise to everyone who is born again. The Holy Spirit strengthens you, keeps you, guides you, warns you of upcoming trouble, gives you power, and helps you to share God's goodness, as well as so much more. Your church and pastor will instruct you on how to receive the Holy Spirit. You can also read in your Bible all of the scriptures on the Holy Spirit (also called the Holy Ghost), especially John 14-16.

*Witness*—tell others of the goodness of Jesus. Help someone else find Him. Tell what He has done for you. Don't beat others over the head with the Bible; simply share His love! Invite them to church with you. God will meet them just where they are. It is our duty, as born again believers, to bring others into His kingdom.

*Allow Jesus to change your life.* Let God make you and mold you through prayer, praise, giving, and through hearing the anointed Word of God. It won't be easy, but it will be worth it!

*Confess your sins.* After being born again, there are times in our Christian walk that we fall prey to temptation and sin. Because of the invincible seed—our new genetic traits—we should not be comfortable with sin. Remember 1 John 5:4? "For everyone born of God overcomes the world. This is the victory that has overcome the world, even our faith. Who is it that overcomes the world? Only he who believes that Jesus is the Son of God."

*Allow God into your life.* God has called you for a divine purpose. Your life has new meaning now that you are born again. That's why He has called *you* out of the darkness into His light. Your life will never be the same! However, saying some words is not enough; you must allow Him to change your life.

Remember, God has already deposited in you many gifts and talents. Use them for His glory! Your gift or talent may be singing, teaching, or visiting the sick. These things alone—works—will not save you, but they are ways to show God thanks, and often. Give yourself to expanding the Kingdom—whether it be your time, service, money, resources, prayer, or experience.

God will take your little and turn it into much. He's not looking for your ability but your *availability*. Tell Him, "Lord, I'm available to You!" and give Him the glory!

## Conclusion

You were born to overcome. In you lies the invincible seed of your Father, the Lord God Almighty. The Lord is mighty in battle and will deliver you. He is the King of Kings, the Lord of Lords, the Alpha and Omega, the Beginning and the End, and He's the author and finisher of our faith. He has started a good work in you and is faithful to complete it!

*He who has an ear, let him hear what the Spirit says to the churches. To him who overcomes, I will give the right to eat from the tree of life, which is in the paradise of God.*
Revelation 2:7

*To him who overcomes and does my will to the end, I will give authority over the nations.*
Revelation 2:26

*To him who overcomes, I will give the right to sit with me on my throne, just as I overcame and sat down with my Father on his throne.*
Revelation 3:21

# Works Cited

Abraham, Ken. *The King and the Beast*. Nashville, Tennessee: Thomas Nelson Publishers, 1991.

Biracree, Tom. *Wilma Rudolph*. New York, New Haven, Philadelphia: Chelsea House Publishers, 1988.

Brown, Les. *Live Your Dreams*. New York: William Morrow and Company, Inc., 1992.

Krantz, Rachel. *The Biographical Dictionary of Black Americans*. New York: Facts on File, 1992.

Wilson, Beth P. *Stevie Wonder*. New York: G.P. Putnam's Sons, 1979.

*The Light Sword Bible*. KJV- Amplified Parallel Bible. Grand Rapids, MI: Zondervan Publishing House, 1993.

Chand, Samuel R. *Failure: The Womb of Success*. Enumclaw, WA: WinePress Publishing, 1999.

# Author Contact Information

For more information please contact:

Pastor Wiley Jackson, Jr.
P.O. Box 18115
Atlanta, GA 30316

Phone: (404) 370-3800
Website: www.wordinaction.info